BUILDING A WEALTHY MINDSET

Unlocking the Secrets to Financial Freedom and Abundance

SAMUEL DANIEL

DEDICATION

To God, the Owner and Director of my life;

To everyone who aspires to bless lives with their wealth, and;

To my loving, adorable, and beautiful wife, Oluwaseun Deborah, who encourages me to impact lives positively, this book is humbly dedicated.

TABLE OF CONTENTS

DEDICATION — iv

TABLE OF CONTENTS — v

INTRODUCTION — 8

CHAPTER 1 — 10

UNDERSTANDING WEALTH — 10

From Scarcity to Abundance — 12

Money Management and Wealth Creation — 12

Myths and Misconceptions about Wealth — 14

CHAPTER 2 — 19

THE POWER OF MINDSET — 19

Impact of Mindset on Wealth — 20

Cultivating an Abundance Mindset — 20

Belief and Financial Decisions — 23

Cultivating Positive Financial Beliefs — 24

Instilling the Wealthy Mindset in Daily Life — 26

CHAPTER 3 — 27

GOAL-SETTING FOR WEALTH CREATION — 27

The SMART Criteria — 27

Create an Action Plan — 30

Tracking Your Progress — 31

Develop a Support System — 31

CHAPTER 4   **33**

FINANCIAL LITERACY AND EDUCATION 33

Fundamental Concepts of Financial Literacy 34

The Role of Education in Financial Literacy 35

Overcoming Barriers to Financial Literacy   37

CHAPTER 5   **39**

BUILDING MULTIPLE INCOME STREAMS

                                                 39

Why Build Multiple Income Streams?   40

Types of Income Streams   41

Strategies for Investing Wisely   42

CHAPTER 6   **47**

THE ROLE OF RISK AND FAILURE   **47**

Understanding Risk   47

Embracing Calculated Risks   48

The Fear of Failure   48

Learning from Failure   49

Risk and Failure in the Journey to Wealth   50

Resilience and Persistence in the Face of
Setbacks

CHAPTER 7   **53**

NETWORKING AND MENTORSHIP   **53**

Building Relationships   54

Finding the Right Mentor   55

Leveraging relationships for financial growth 57

CHAPTER 8   **59**

PHILANTHROPY AND GIVING BACK   **59**

Philanthropy- An Extension of Wealth   60

Creating a Legacy   60

Cultivating a Culture of Giving   62

CHAPTER 9   **68**

WEALTH AND WELL-BEING   **68**

Understanding Wealth Beyond Money   68

The Psychology of Wealth and Well-Being   70

Practical Steps Toward Integrating Wealth and Well-Being   70

Importance of Health and Happiness   72

The Wealth of Health   72

The Pursuit of Happiness   73

The Synergy of Health, Happiness, and Wealth   74

CHAPTER 10   **76**

MAINTAINING WEALTH   **76**

Establishing a Growth-Oriented Financial Strategy   77

CONCLUSION   **79**

INTRODUCTION

With an increasing desire for riches, many often misinterpret wealth as simply the accumulation of money and possessions. However, the valid key to prosperity transcends the external paraphernalia of success to individuals' mindsets. *"Building a Wealthy Mindset: Unlocking the Secrets to Financial Freedom and Abundance"* actuates the potency of your thoughts and beliefs. Moreover, it demystifies the traditional notions and myths of wealth creation.

Instead of tailoring your imagination to failure, littleness, and poverty, envision waking up each day not burdened by the weight of financial insecurity. You can be invigorated by a clear vision of abundance. As you envisage navigating through life with unswerving confidence, your imagination will lead you to make pragmatic decisions that enhance financial stability.

This book explores the fundamental principles that govern a wealthy mentality. It exposes how to harness the transformative power of positive thinking, develop resilience during adversity, and become dogged while aligning your actions with your goals. Furthermore, this book unpacks the myths inhibiting your progress and provides strategies for dismantling limiting beliefs that have unconsciously maneuvered your life.

"Wealthy Mindset" is your roadmap to unlock your full potential. Beyond a guide to financial prosperity, this book is a call to arms for anyone desiring greater happiness, fulfilment, and significance.

This book will transform your thoughts and shift your perspective as you embark on a life-changing odyssey. I trust you are set to awaken the power within you and redefine what true wealth means. Prepare for a mind shift as your journey to a wealthier life begins.

CHAPTER 1

UNDERSTANDING WEALTH

Commonly, wealth is associated with abundance in terms of financial and material riches. However, true wealth encapsulates much more than just a robust bank account. It is the conglomeration of economic security, personal fulfilment, emotional well-being, and social connectedness.

Several wealthy individuals understand that their financial status is only one aspect of their wealth. They often develop a rich and holistic life experience that includes purposeful work, strong relationships, and a balanced lifestyle. Without such balance, life could be miserable with much financial or material resources.

Many people are well-to-do financially but lack peace and social connection. Such people derive little or no satisfaction from their money. Therefore, understanding the various aspects of wealth has a significant implication. It will help you develop the proper sense of self-judgment. Let's go through multiple spheres of wealth.

Financial Wealth is the most recognised form of wealth. It encompasses savings, investments, properties, and income streams. It also provides the money to acquire goods, services, and experiences that promote one's quality of life.

Emotional Wealth. Emotional stability plays a significant role in building a wealthy mindset. Healing from past ordeals, managing stress, and building resilience all contribute to a meaningful life. It is proven that individuals who are emotionally rich tend to cultivate positive relationships and maintain a healthy mindset toward wealth creation.

Social wealth refers to the quality of our relationships and social networks. People who build supportive communities and engage in meaningful connections with others increase their overall happiness and sense of belonging. Relationships will always remain a currency. Whatever money can purchase, a good relationship can equally provide. Besides, life is miserable for anyone who is financially rich but relationally poor.

Time Wealth: True wealth offers you the luxury of choosing how you spend your time. The wealth of time allows individuals to prioritise and manage their personal interests, family commitments, and self-care without the constant pressure of financial constraints. Wealthy individuals only leverage time to amass their possessions.

Poor people might remain impoverished until they learn to prioritise the wealth of time available to them. Fair enough, we all have 24 hours per day and 7 days per week. Time is the only equitable wealth to all, but our priorities make it appear that some have more time than others.

From Scarcity to Abundance

The greatest barrier to developing a wealthy mindset is the prevalent scarcity mentality. This notion is fueled by the false idea that one must struggle to attain financial success because resources are limited and available to only a particular group. This mindset often leads to fear, anxiety, and lack of initiative.

Conversely, an abundance mentality is the belief that opportunities abound and success can be collective. It would be great if everyone got rid of their hustling mentality and positioned their minds to maximise the untapped resources and opportunities around them.

Money Management and Wealth Creation

Effective money management and investing will be upheld with an accurate understanding of wealth. Wealthy individuals acknowledge that their financial resources are tools they must utilise wisely. Let's find out some basic principles of money management and wealth creation:

Budgeting. Creating a budget helps you to track your income and expenses. It aids you in making informed financial decisions that align with your long-term goals. You should evaluate how you have been spending your income. You could be surprised that 70% of your income is squandered.

Investments. It is called investment when you allocate resources into various investment vehicles that can foster long-term returns through compound interest and capital growth. However, it is crucial to understand risk tolerance and diversification. More so, avoid "get-rich-quick" schemes. Only those who sell those ideas make their filthy lucre from them. So, be sure to do your research and invest wisely.

Passive Income. This sort of income stream can be done without active, ongoing effort. Many wealthy individuals leverage passive income to build fortunes for themselves. This allows for greater financial freedom and additional time to pursue personal interests or investments.

Myths and Misconceptions about Wealth

Several individuals view wealth through the lens of glitz and glamour. For them, wealth is building mansions, driving luxury cars, and going for extravagant vacations. As good as those things are, they are peripheral to success.

Behind the surface of wealth lies a complex interplay of beliefs, behaviours, and realities that can propagate myths and misconceptions about what true wealth means. Understanding these myths will help you navigate your financial journeys more clearly and purposefully.

Myth 1: Wealth Equals Happiness

One of the most prevalent myths is the ideology that wealth directly translates to happiness. Although financial stability can help in alleviating stresses related to basic needs and security, research shows that after attaining a certain income level, marginal revenue does little to increase overall happiness.

Multiple factors influence emotional well-being, including relationships, purpose, and personal fulfilment. Therefore, equating wealth with happiness can be highly misleading, as individuals chase after money in the hope that it will solve their deeper emotional needs. Victims of this myth have found that after making money, the vacuum in their lives remains unfilled.

Myth 2: Rich People Are Bad

There is the stereotype that wealthy individuals are greedy or unethical. While some wealthy people may engage in unethical practices, it's essential to understand that wealth does not inherently corrupt people's character. Many wealthy individuals contribute significantly to society through philanthropy, volunteerism, and mentorship.

Moreover, the belief that wealth accumulation only stems from exploitation can overshadow the hard work, innovation, and strategic decision-making that often accompany wealth creation. Unethical behaviours spring from character deficiency, not from wealth amassed. In short, poverty tends to make people more brutal than wealth. This is evident in third-world countries, where the highest security threats are found.

Myth 3: You Must Inherit Wealth to Be Rich

Another prevalent myth is that wealth is primarily inherited. Although families sometimes pass down financial assets, the reality is that most of the wealthiest people in our world today amass their fortunes through entrepreneurship, investing, or career advancement.

Many self-made millionaires come from humble backgrounds but are driven by ambition, discipline, and a willingness to learn from failures. This implies that wealth is attainable for anyone willing to commit to their financial education and personal growth.

Myth 4: The Wealthy Don't Work Hard

Contrary to the belief that wealthy individuals coast through life effortlessly, many have achieved their status through years of hard work, persistence, and dedication. Today, "working smarter, not harder" often surfaces in discussions about wealth, but that can be a half-truth. Acknowledging that most successful people have invested countless hours into developing their careers and honing their skills is essential. The narrative of the "lazy rich" is not a bone for any serious-minded individual to chew. Whatever oversimplifies the journey to financial independence and overlooks personal sacrifices is worth fleeing from.

Myth 5: Money Can Buy Everything

Indeed, money guarantees access to countless resources and opportunities. However, it cannot buy everything. For instance, money cannot purchase love, respect, and genuine relationships. Wealth can facilitate experiences, but true fulfilment is engendered through meaningful value-adding connections with others.

Furthermore, pursuing material possessions can lead to what is known as "hedonic adaptation," a situation in which an individual quickly becomes accustomed to their newfound wealth and increasingly desires more to achieve the same level of satisfaction.

Myth 6: Financial Success Is About Luck

The idea that wealth is a descendant of luck or chance downplays the role of hard work, strategic planning, and informed decision-making in building financial success. While it's possible to experience sudden windfalls or unprecedented opportunities, most individuals who make substantial wealth do so through consistent effort, strategic investments, and a grounded understanding of their financial environment.

The danger of this misconception is that it can create a passive mindset that can lead individuals to complacency. Instead of pursuing their financial goals, they be resort to waiting for luck.

Understanding the myths and misconceptions about wealth is essential to empower you to redefine your relationship with money. As you dispel these myths, focus on a more holistic approach to financial well-being. Ensure that the pursuit of economic success is balanced with ethical responsibility, personal growth, and meaningful connections.

In its most enriching form, wealth transcends keeping a robust bank account. It is a pathway to greater opportunities for ourselves and those around us.

As we progress in this book, we will unravel practical strategies and insights that will empower you to reshape your understanding of wealth and, ultimately, your financial destiny. Now is the time to embrace a more nuanced understanding of what true wealth entails.

CHAPTER 2

THE POWER OF MINDSET

At its core, mindset refers to an individual's beliefs, motivations, and attitudes. It mirrors how we perceive ourselves, the world, and what we believe is possible. Simply put, your mindset is what you set your mind to think or achieve.

Psychology researcher Carol Dweck distinguished between two mindsets—a fixed mindset and a growth mindset. He explains that a fixed mindset sees intelligence, talent, and skills as static and unchangeable, leading individuals to shy away from challenges and fear failure. In sharp contrast, a growth mindset embraces challenges, views failures as learning opportunities, and believes in the power of effort and persistence.

This means that our mindset determines the outcome of every situation we encounter. For instance, although failure is an outcome, it can result in two different dispositions based on different mindsets. Whereas one individual can accept failure as the end of the road, another could perceive it as the beginning of a new route.

Impact of Mindset on Wealth

The mindset you adopt plays a critical role in how you approach wealth. People with wealthy mindsets are often characterised by optimism, resilience, and a strong belief in their ability to learn and adapt. This positive perception gears people to take proactive steps toward financial success. With the right mindset, you are not afraid of challenges or setbacks. Instead, you discern them as stepping stones on the path to achieving your goals.

Research has shown that mindset significantly impacts financial decision-making. For instance, individuals with a growth mindset are more likely to seek out financial education, take calculated risks, and invest in their personal development. This is because they understand that acquiring wealth is a journey that requires continuous learning and adaptation.

Cultivating an Abundance Mindset

Your first step towards abundance is gratitude. Acknowledging what you have rather than focusing on what you lack can shift your perspective towards abundance. Start a gratitude journal and jot down three things you appreciate each day.

People who only grumble and complain about their circumstances will hardly find a way out. But being grateful for the little you have unburdens and redirects your heart to newer possibilities. If you don't have much to be thankful for right now, envision what you desire to achieve and start showing gratitude for what is coming your way.

Second, go for knowledge. Open yourself to continuous learning and self-improvement. Embrace challenges as growth opportunities rather than viewing them as obstacles. "Knowledge is power," they say. The more knowledge you acquire, the more equipped and empowered you are to make wealth.

Knowledge is empowering. Read books, attend seminars, and seek mentorship in personal finance. Each new piece of information can reshape your understanding and approach to wealth.

Third, collaboration. Work together with others to share knowledge, experiences, and resources. Collaboration opens doors and fosters a sense of community. Always think of succeeding with others. A lone mentality is enough prison to hold one captive in penury.

Your environment significantly impacts your mindset. Engage with individuals who inspire you and share a similar vision for financial success. Their positivity and achievements can motivate you to pursue your goals.

Fourth, challenge limiting beliefs. Identify any negative beliefs you hold about money. Do you think rich people are greedy? Challenge that thought and replace it with the idea that wealth can be used as a tool for good.

Fifth, visualise your success. Use visualisation techniques to imagine your financial goals. What does your life look like with financial freedom? This exercise can reinforce your commitment and clarify your objectives.

The impact of a wealthy mindset extends beyond financial success. It can improve your overall well-being, foster meaningful relationships, and increase your ability to adapt in the face of obstacles. As you internalise a mindset of abundance, you'll find yourself making bolder decisions, pursuing opportunities with greater confidence, and engaging a network of supportive individuals.

Moreover, as you evolve, your wealth will be not only reflected in financial terms but also the richness of life experiences and personal fulfilment. A wealthy mindset also encourages generosity, thus creating a cycle of abundance that benefits you and those within your circle.

Belief and Financial Decisions

Our beliefs shape our decisions and determine the extent to which we can take steps that can lead to financial freedom or slavery. I will highlight some of the ways our beliefs affect our financial decisions, either directly or indirectly.

Risk Tolerance. Our beliefs about money often dictate how much risk we are willing to take. For instance, individuals who believe they are financially prudent may be more inclined to invest in stocks or start a business. They may esteem these actions as learning opportunities.

Conversely, people who doubt their financial acumen might prefer safer, more traditional routes like savings accounts or government bonds, potentially limiting their financial growth.

Attracting Opportunities. Belief also influences our perception of opportunities. Positive beliefs about wealth and success can attract better job prospects, lucrative investments, and networking connections. Though arguable, the Law of Attraction suggests that a positive mindset can create a magnetic pull toward opportunities aligned with one's beliefs. Individuals who believe they are worthy of financial success find themselves in the right place at the right time. People will always move in the direction of their belief system, whether by attraction or what have you.

Handling Setbacks. Financial journeys are never a straight path; failures and challenges are part of the package. However, beliefs about failure determine how one responds to these challenges. Individuals with a resilient belief system are more likely to learn from mistakes and adapt. In contrast, someone with a negative belief may spiral into despair and disengagement, worsening their financial situation.

Spending and Saving Habits. Our beliefs about money significantly shape our attitudes toward spending and saving. Someone who perceives money as a limited resource may hoard rather than invest or spend, which could hamper potential opportunities. Conversely, those who see money as a tool for growth are more willing to invest in themselves, whether through education or business opportunities; they recognise the potential for future returns.

Cultivating Positive Financial Beliefs

Generally, we are more prone to believe negativity than positivity. This is why developing positive beliefs should be encouraged. It requires more effort to cultivate a positive mindset than it does to be pessimistic. However, developing positive beliefs is highly enriching; it is worth all the effort, time, resources, and alignment you may need to invest in it. Here are practical strategies to build a positive financial belief system:

1. **Education and Awareness**: Financial literacy can help reshape beliefs about money. Learning fundamental principles of creating a budget, investing, and managing debt will empower you to approach your finances confidently.

2. **Surrounding Ourselves with Positive Influences**: The people we associate with can impact our beliefs. Connect yourself to a network of financially savvy individuals who can guide you, boost your confidence, and help reshape negative beliefs about money.

3. **Setting Achievable Goals**: Never rush to make it big; only plan towards it. Begin with small financial goals that are not only realistic but also attainable. Also, learn to encourage yourself by celebrating small successes. As you do, you will find encouragement to tackle greater financial challenges over time.

Instilling the Wealthy Mindset in Daily Life

Consistency is vital to making a wealthy mindset a part of your everyday life. Incorporate mindfulness practices such as meditation or journaling to reflect on your thoughts and progress. Regularly engage with materials that inspire and motivate you, such as books, podcasts, or videos related to wealth creation and personal development.

Surround yourself with individuals who exemplify a wealthy mindset and emulate them. Also, engage in conversations that stimulate and encourage growth, and be open to giving and receiving constructive feedback. Always remember that developing a wealthy mindset requires intentional practice and commitment to living with purpose and positivity.

A correct mindset is a lifelong learning, discovery, and adaptation journey. As you continue to cultivate your wealthy mindset, keep in mind that the greatest changes often occur within. Eventually, these changes will shape both your financial destiny and your entire life experience.

CHAPTER 3

GOAL-SETTING FOR WEALTH CREATION

A goal is the compass that leads you to the outcome you envision. Since wealth does not depend solely on developing the right mindset, goal-setting is the bridge that connects an abundance mindset to tangible outcomes. Without clearly defined objectives, it will be very difficult, if not impossible, to shape our financial futures. Setting goals provides direction, fosters motivation, and helps us be accountable.

The SMART Criteria

Adhering to the SMART criteria, a widely recognised framework that enhances the probability of successful goal attainment is crucial to effectively setting wealth-oriented goals. SMART stands for Specific, Measurable, Achievable, Relevant, and Time-bound.

Specific. Your goals should be clearly defined to avoid ambiguity. For example, instead of aiming to "save money," a particular goal would be, "I want to save $10,000 for a down payment on a house."

When your aim is ambiguous and vague, you may find yourself without a clear target. Many times, unspecified goals amount to a waste of time and effort. Don't just set a goal; make sure it is specific and defined.

Measurable. It is essential to establish criteria to measure your progress. For instance, break down the savings goal into monthly targets, such as saving $1000 monthly.

Note that the example is just a guide. You may save more or less. What is more important is that you set goals that can be measured progressively. You should be able to tell how many percentages of success you have achieved as you progress.

Achievable. Goals should be realistic and attainable. To sustain your motivation, ensure that your goal is grounded in reality. Assess your current financial situation and set a target that challenges you yet remains possible to attain.

Many set goals that are unachievable because they are overzealous. For instance, don't save a higher percentage of your income without planning for essential budgets. Doing so could make your financial goals unachievable. If you earn $1000 per month and decide to save $900, it becomes clear that you will hardly achieve such a goal.

Relevant: Each goal you set should align with both your financial aspirations and life ambitions. A goal may be excellent but irrelevant. An honest question to ask yourself is: "How does achieving this goal contribute to my long-term wealth strategy?"

In the foregoing example, if you have chosen to save a specific amount of money monthly, you should also state the money's relevance to your overall financial pursuit. That makes the goal relevant.

Time-bound. Don't spend eternity pursuing a goal. Setting deadlines is crucial to foster urgency. For example, "I want to save $10,000 between December 2024 and December 2025." Your one-year timeline helps maintain focus and encourages consistent action.

Setting a time frame allows you to spread your goals across time intervals. You could divide the total amount you wish to save by December 31, 2025, by the number of months you have before the deadline. Again, setting time limits for your goals helps you stay focused and diligent. However, always ensure that your goals are achievable within your set time frame.

Once your goals are set, visualisation can further empower your journey towards wealth creation. Spend time regularly picturing yourself achieving your financial objectives. Visualising success motivates and enables you to harness the emotional energy required to attain your goals.

Create an Action Plan

A goal without an action plan is merely a dream. Although several people archive their goals in a journal, they don't take any active steps towards achieving them. Such people are worse than those who have no vision for their lives because they cannot claim ignorance.

It is highly essential to break down your wealth goals into actionable steps. This means you must identify the actions required to record a breakthrough. Now, if your goal is to invest in stocks, your action plan could include tasks such as:

- Researching investment platforms

- Educating yourself about stock market basics

- Setting a monthly budget for investments

- Consulting with a financial advisor

Breaking your goals into actionable steps will help you achieve success. Moreover, your goals will inform and guide your daily actions.

Tracking Your Progress

Monitoring your progress allows for adjustments along the way. Review your goals and action plans regularly to assess your progress. This practice keeps you accountable and also provides the opportunity to celebrate small victories, thereby instilling positive behaviours that contribute to success.

Additionally, if you fail in any area, use it as an opportunity to readjust your strategies. The hallmark of a prosperous mindset is the flexibility to adapt. Never see setbacks as stumbling blocks; embrace them as learning experiences.

Develop a Support System

Every genuine wealth features a community of like-minded people. To attain wealth, the connections you forge must be carefully considered. Surrounding yourself with like-minded individuals who share similar financial goals or values can provide encouragement and support. It would be great if you joined financial groups or online platforms where members share their progress and offer tips and strategies for wealth creation. With a support network, you can gain fresh ideas and be accountable.

To conclude this chapter, be reminded of the principles of effective goal-setting and the significance of clarity and planning in your financial journey. Ensure your goals are SMART, create actionable plans, track your progress, build a support system, and visualise success.

Furthermore, remember that a wealthy mindset is not only about acquiring money; holistically, it is about creating a life of abundance. With actionable goals and a resolute spirit, you will achieve the wealth you desire.

CHAPTER 4

FINANCIAL LITERACY AND EDUCATION

Understanding financial literacy and prioritising money management is crucial to building a abundance mindset. In this chapter, we shall consider the essential concepts of financial literacy, explore their impact on personal wealth accumulation, and provide practical steps for enhancing financial knowledge.

Financial literacy refers to understanding and applying various financial skills, including personal financial management, budgeting, and investing. Every wealthy individual builds their financial future on these fundamental principles. A wealthier mindset begins with acknowledging that financial literacy is not optional but essential to navigating today's financial complexities.

The effects of financial ignorance can be severe. For instance, poor financial decisions can result in debt, wasted efforts, and missed opportunities. Conversely, financial literacy empowers individuals to make wise decisions and maximise their potential for wealth creation. More so, financial knowledge ensures stability in both personal and professional lives.

Fundamental Concepts of Financial Literacy

Let's share the most important concepts of financial literacy as we attempt to strengthen our mindset for wealth creation.

1. **Budgeting**: A budget serves as a guidepost for your financial journey. By creating and sticking to a budget, you can track your income and expenditures more easily. Budgeting helps you live within your means of earning and prepares you for unexpected expenses.

2. **Saving and Emergency Funds**: Accumulating savings and preparing an emergency fund are crucial for financial security. Savings and emergency funds are safety nets that provide peace of mind and help prevent individuals from falling into debt due to unforeseen circumstances.

3. **Debt Management**: Different types of debt exist, such as credit cards, student loans, and mortgages. Correct debt management is vital to wealth creation. Debt management helps

you delineate between good debt, which can help build wealth, and bad debt, which can lead to financial ruin.

4. **Investing**: This is engaging your money or asset to yield profitable returns. To become financially stable, you must learn how to make your money work through various investment schemes such as bonds, stocks, and real estate. The earlier you begin to invest, the more you can benefit from compound interest. This allows you to maximise your financial growth over time.

5. **Retirement Planning**: It is never too early to start planning for retirement if you don't want to spend your old age doing hard labour. Adequate understanding of retirement accounts, such as IRAs and 401(k)s, and the benefits of employer matching can significantly boost your financial future.

The Role of Education in Financial Literacy

Education is the bedrock of financial literacy. We live in an age where information is at our disposal. Unfortunately, many lack ample knowledge on how to develop their economic lives. Here are some valuable resources for developing financial knowledge:

1. **Formal Education**: Enroll in finance-related courses through traditional schooling or online platforms that can provide structured learning. In today's world, economics, personal finance, and investing are priceless.

2. **Books and Literature**: Several literatures are dedicated to financial literacy. For example, classics such as "Rich Dad Poor Dad" by Robert Kiyosaki and "The Total Money Makeover" by Dave Ramsey provide insightful and practical advice that can change one's financial mindset.

3. **Mentorship**: We must emphasize the significance of mentorship in the journey to financial stability. Learning from those who are financially successful can provide insights that formal education may not. Find a versatile mentor in financial management and accelerate your learning as you draw motivation from them.

4. **Workshops and Seminars**: Attending workshops or financial seminars offer hands-on learning experiences. These events often cover essential topics, allowing for interactive sessions and networking opportunities.

5. **Online Resources and Tools**: Several podcasts, websites, and apps are dedicated to enhancing financial literacy and can help people learn at their own pace. For instance, Coursera, Khan Academy, and other financial websites provide valuable resources for anyone willing to learn. Besides, LinkedIn, Fiverr, and other social platforms offer remote job opportunities.

Overcoming Barriers to Financial Literacy

Despite the recognised importance of financial literacy, several people still face barriers to accessing financial education. These barriers may include socioeconomic status, insufficient resources, or negative previous experiences with financial institutions.

However, you must not give up your pursuit of true wealth. Community programs and nonprofit organisations currently offer free or low-cost financial education to deal with these obstacles. Most schools are also beginning to incorporate financial literacy into their curriculums to ensure that future generations are better equipped to handle their finances.

Beyond amassing wealth, developing a wealthy mindset requires understanding the dynamics of money, making wise financial decisions, and continuously learning. Prioritising financial literacy lays the foundation for financial independence and growth. Moreover, embracing education and adjusting to new financial knowledge is the key to amassing lasting wealth.

CHAPTER 5

BUILDING MULTIPLE INCOME STREAMS

With the current economic meltdown and ever-increasing inflation, relying on a single source of income can be risky. This Chapter explores one of the key principles of financial success: building multiple income streams. This strategy not only promotes financial security but also fast-tracks wealth accumulation and independence.

Multiple income streams are the practice of expanding one's sources of income beyond a conventional job or salary. These varying sources of income can stem from various activities like investments or businesses. By building a multiple income stream, one creates a buffer against economic downturns and sudden life changes. This principle puts one in charge of one's financial future and allows for a more flexible approach to wealth creation.

Why Build Multiple Income Streams?

1. **Financial Security**: Depending solely on one job can leave you vulnerable. Job loss, illness, or economic downturn can disrupt your income flow badly. However, you mitigate this risk by creating marginal revenue sources.

2. **Accelerated Wealth Growth**: Multiple streams mean multiple opportunities for earning. Each new income source contributes to your overall wealth, allowing you to achieve your financial goals.

3. **Personal and Professional Growth**: You will develop personally as you explore different income-generating avenues. You will learn new skills, broaden your horizons, and even develop a new career path aligning with your passions.

4. **Enhanced Financial Independence**: Multiple income streams offer you the liberty to make choices not entirely influenced by financial necessity. Whether you are pursuing a passion project, travelling, or taking some rest, this independence is priceless.

Types of Income Streams

There are various categories of income streams; however, each has its unique advantages and challenges. Here are the major types to consider:

1. **Active income** is the most available form of income in which you exchange time for money. Examples include your primary job, freelancing, teaching, or consulting. Although active income provides a stable cash flow, it is limited to the number of hours you can work.

2. **Passive Income**: This income requires an initial investment of time or resources, but in the long run, it generates income with little or no ongoing effort. Some good examples of passive income streams are royalties from books or music, rental properties, stock dividends, and revenue from online courses.

3. **Portfolio Income**: This form of income stream is generated from investments like bonds, stocks, and real estate, and it provides regular cash flow through interest, dividends, or capital gains. However, it requires a good understanding of investment strategies and market dynamics.

4. **Entrepreneurial Income**: Starting a business is a great way to generate additional income. Although entrepreneurship comes with its risks and challenges, it allows for creative expression and has the potential for a high profit on investment.

Strategies for Investing Wisely

Investing can be a powerful means to build wealth and secure financial stability. However, it's crucial to approach investing with a strategy to mitigate risks and enhance your chances of success. Below are several methods to help you invest wisely and make decisions that resonate with your financial goals.

1. Set Clear Financial Goals

Before you start investing, ensure you define your financial objectives. Whether you are saving for retirement, planning for a child's education, or aiming to buy a home, goal-setting will guide your investment decisions. Creating a timeline for these goals will also help you discover your risk tolerance and the nature of suitable investments.

2. Understand Your Risk Tolerance

Every investor has a different comfort level with risk. Risk tolerance is mostly influenced by age, financial situation, investment knowledge, and how you react to market fluctuations. Therefore, understanding your risk tolerance will guide you in choosing investments that align with your comfort level and financial goals.

3. Diversify Your Portfolio

Diversification is one of the key principles of wise investing. It involves spreading your investments across various asset classes (stocks, bonds, mutual funds, real estate, etc.) to minimise risk. More so, diversification helps mitigate the impact of a poor-performing asset on your overall investments. This strategy offers you the opportunity to take advantage of different performance trends across different sectors and industries.

4. Invest for the Long Term

Based on short-term fluctuations, most investors are tempted to make impulsive decisions because of market volatility. However, successful investments usually require long-term trends. Historical data reveals that, despite periodic downturns, markets mostly rise over extended periods. By holding long-term investments, you can benefit from compound growth and minimise the effects of short-term market fluctuations.

5. Educate Yourself about Investment Products

Knowledge is crucial when it comes to investing. So, you must familiarise yourself with different investment options, including bonds, stocks, ETFs, mutual funds, and real estate. Each investment platform has its advantages and risks. Understanding these dynamics will help you make informed decisions and tailor your strategy to your financial goals.

6. Consider Dollar-Cost Averaging

Dollar-cost averaging is a strategy where you disregard market conditions to invest a fixed amount of money at regular intervals. This approach balances the impact of market volatility, as you purchase more shares when prices are low and fewer when prices skyrocket. Over time, this can lead to a lower average cost per share and potentially increase your returns.

7. Regularly Review and Rebalance Your Portfolio

Investment performance can evolve over time and may result in imbalances. By regularly reviewing your investments, you ensure they remain in alignment with your goals and risk tolerance. You can also decide to rebalance your portfolio by selling overperforming assets and buying underperforming ones. Thus, you can maintain your desired asset and heighten your profits.

8. Be Cautious of Market Timing

Many investors fall victim to trying to time the market, buying or selling based on short-term predictions. While making decisions based on current market trends can be tempting, timing the market is highly unpredictable. Instead, focus on your long-term investment strategy and avoid making rash decisions based on temporary market conditions.

9. Stay Informed but Avoid Information Overload

Get up-to-date information about market trends and economic factors that drive your investments. However, more information can lead to clarity and strong decision-making. Find a balance by maintaining reputable sources of financial news and analysis while staying on course with your long-term goals.

10. Consult with a Financial Advisor

If you need clarification about how to proceed with your investments, it is highly recommended that you consider consulting with a financial advisor. A qualified advisor can guide your unique financial situation and goals. More so, a good advisor can help you develop a comprehensive investment strategy, monitor your progress, and adjust your plan should such a need arise.

Undoubtedly, building multiple income streams is an essential step toward wealth creation. By diversifying your income sources, you are preparing your route to financial security and independence and building your potential for wealth accumulation. As you implement the strategies discussed in this chapter, keep in mind that patience and persistence are the keys to unlocking lasting wealth.

CHAPTER 6

THE ROLE OF RISK AND FAILURE

In pursuing wealth and success, two factors frequently emerge as obstacles and opportunities: risk and failure. Beyond mere hindrances on the path to financial abundance, these two elements are integral to developing a wealthy mindset. This chapter will explore how embracing risk and learning from failure can lead to greater achievements and a more profound understanding of financial prosperity.

Understanding Risk

Risk is a fundamental aspect of life and business. It refers to the potential for loss or uncertainty regarding an investment's future returns. In financial terms, risk is often quantified, assessed, and sometimes feared. However, it is essential to reconstruct this perspective; risk can also be seen as an opportunity for growth and wealth creation.

Wealthy individuals, from entrepreneurs to investors, often thrive in uncertain environments. They recognise that high rewards typically come with high risks. Conversely, those who avoid risk may miss opportunities leading to significant financial gain. Thus, developing a wealthy mindset begins with understanding and accepting that risk is inherent in any venture.

Embracing Calculated Risks

While risks are unavoidable, not all risks are wise. Successful individuals distinguish between calculated risks and reckless gambles. Calculated risks involve analysis, research, and strategic planning. They are informed decisions made after considering the potential outcomes and consequences.

As an individual aiming to cultivate a prosperous mindset, it is crucial to become comfortable with taking calculated risks. This might involve investing in stocks, pursuing entrepreneurial endeavours, or exploring new markets. Education and experience play critical roles in identifying which risks are worth taking. A wealthy mindset thrives on informed action rather than mere chance.

The Fear of Failure

For the vast majority, failure is perceived negatively. Consequently, they are imprisoned by the fear of risk and chained with hesitation. However, people with wealthy mindsets have a different perspective; they view failure as an opportunity to improve rather than a setback. In business and finance, failure is commonplace. It is a critical feedback loop that offers insights for future decisions and strategies.

It helps to understand that failure does not reflect one's abilities. Instead, see it as a powerful realisation that you need to improve and strive more for success. Every setback presents a disguised opportunity for growth, innovation, and development. So, stop esteeming wealthy individuals as people who never fail or experience challenges. Instead, see them as individuals whose failures shape their journeys and lead them to redefine their strategies and approaches.

Learning from Failure

The ability to learn from failure is the hallmark of a flourishing mindset. Instead of wallowing in regret, analyse your failures and learn from them. Try to examine what went wrong, identify your errors, and make amends where necessary. As you learn from your mistakes and failures, you will minimise the likelihood of repeating mistakes and hone your decision-making skills.

Furthermore, the more you learn and deal with failures, the more resilient you will become. As one aspiring to become wealthy, you should understand that persistence in adversity is essential for success.

So, develop a mindset that pictures challenges as opportunities for evolution. Then, you can quickly bounce back stronger and become more determined than ever.

Risk and Failure in the Journey to Wealth

Risk and failure are essential components in the journey to wealth. They are not endpoints, as some people believe. Do you know that the most successful people in our world shine in environments where others fail? This happens because individuals with wealthy mindsets take calculated risks that others fear, and when they encounter failure, they transform those experiences into lessons learned.

Every wealthy mindset embraces this dynamic relationship between risk and failure. They understand that obstacles and setbacks often encounter financial success, but within them lies potential rewards.

Resilience and Persistence in the Face of Setbacks

Every form of success requires resilience and persistence. Many fail to achieve their goals because they want quick results. Eventually, they fall off the wagon of persistent efforts. Contrary to some beliefs that wealth creation is a straightforward journey where you earn money, invest wisely, and watch your finances blossom, there are far greater complications attached.

Challenges and setbacks can make even the most determined individuals question their path and decisions. This is where resilience and persistence play a critical role in delineating success from failure. Once you develop these traits, you are armed to navigate the ups and downs of financial growth with greater confidence.

Setbacks you may encounter while creating wealth can take different forms, such as unexpected expenses, market downturns, job losses, economic recessions, or personal financial mismanagement. These challenges can be highly disheartening, leading to frustration, helplessness, and doubt. For instance, when some investors experience a market crash, they easily panic and sell off assets at ridiculous prices. Similarly, an unplanned expense can claim savings and disrupt investment plans, leading to discouragement.

Regardless of the obstacles you encounter, realise that setbacks are inevitable in the journey to wealth land. This understanding will help build your resilience and persistence in adversity. Besides, your perspective about failure will change dramatically.

Always remember that the absence of setbacks does not define true success, but how well you respond and manage them. Wealthy individuals are able to take calculated risks, learn from failures, and build resilience. In your financial pursuit, note that risk and failure are hurdles you must face. Embrace them, learn from them, and let them guide you toward a richer and more fulfilling life.

CHAPTER 7

NETWORKING AND MENTORSHIP

Several components unite to produce wealth, which is why true prosperity cannot be independent of meaningful social connections. This chapter examines two concepts that are germane to the pursuit of wealth: networking and mentorship. Let's illuminate the synergistic relationship between these elements and how they contribute to the overall development of a wealthy mindset.

Only shallow minds think of networking as exchanging business cards or making small talk at social gatherings. Any form of social integration that does not culminate into a meaningful relationship that can foster mutual growth and opportunities is not a network. We connect with a community of serious-minded individuals not for the fun of it but because we realise that success is rarely achieved in isolation. Instead, it flourishes through the collective energy and resources that others bring into our lives.

Building Relationships

Effective networking begins with the intention to build meaningful relationships. Some strategies to enrich your networking skills are highlighted below:

1. **Be Authentic**. Everyone is drawn to authenticity. Even a cheat wants to relate to someone who is honest. So, build authenticity first. Approach every relationship with a genuine interest in other people's aspirations, stories, and challenges. When people find that you are genuine, you win their trust and open the door to future collaboration.

2. **Listen Actively**: Networking is a coin with two sides—listening and sharing. Learn to pay attention to what others say and show that you value their perspectives. Active listening will help you understand their needs and also allow you to find ways to help them.

3. **Offer Value**: What you bring to the table is what you will be valued for. So, while trying to network, think about how you can provide value to others. For instance, you can provide insights, offer support, or volunteer to serve. Your value will draw valuable people to you and strengthen your connections.

4. **Follow-up**: Building a network is not spontaneous; it takes time. Follow up regularly with people who can help you, either through casual check-ins or congratulating them on their achievements. The more you register your presence, the deeper your connection will be.

5. **Diversify Your Network**: Surround yourself with individuals from different backgrounds and industries. This diversity will open you up to various ideas, perspectives, and innovative ideas that will foster your growth.

Finding the Right Mentor

Mentorship and networking are similar but not the same. Mentorship is a specific arm of networking. Whereas networking expands your circle of influence, mentorship provides guidance and support from those who have walked the path before you. Your relationship with a mentor is direct, and the goal is clear. A mentor can be essential in developing a wealthy mindset; their experiences can accelerate and guide your personal and professional journey.

Let's highlight how to identify and sustain your relationship with your mentor.

1. **Define Your Goals**: Clearly state what you hope to achieve from a mentoring relationship. It could be career advice, advanced knowledge in a specific discipline, or personal development. Your goals will inform your choice of a suitable mentor.

2. **Look within Your Network**: Assess your current network before looking too far away. Sometimes, a potential mentor is someone within your circle or someone you are already acquainted with. The advantage is that you have more access to them than keeping a role model who needs to recognise you or the peculiarity of your goals.

3. **Be Respectful of Their Time**: Serious-minded people don't joke with time or appointments. When seeking out a mentor, be careful not to fail appointments. Respect their commitments and personality. Always appreciate their experience and state why you would want their guidance.

4. **Be Open to Feedback**: When you finally get a mentor, be willing to accept constructive criticism and learn from their experience. A mentor's role is to challenge you and encourage growth. Your openness and

willingness to learn will help you achieve your goals with your mentor.

5. **Cultivate the Relationship**: Like networking, mentorship requires effort. Communicate with your mentor regularly and demonstrate your commitment to the relationship. Show appreciation for their time and insights. This will make them commit themselves to you more and more.

Leveraging relationships for financial growth

Research shows that individuals with mentors have higher chances of achieving their professional goals and higher satisfaction levels in their careers. Here are ways your relationship with a mentor can be of help:

- **Insightful Guidance**: They can help you navigate challenges and avoid common pitfalls in your journey toward success.

- **Accountability**: Mentors can keep you accountable for your goals. They can monitor and ensure you remain focused and motivated.

- **Access to Opportunities**: A mentor can be a gate to several opportunities. They can introduce you to key players in your area of interest, which could fast-tract your financial journey.

Networking and mentorship are indispensable tools in your pursuit of lasting wealth. The two components create a reliable support system that nurtures growth, learning, and opportunity. You will not make it a personal endeavour if you desire to journey far into wealth. Connecting with those who have successfully navigated the path before you can unlock new possibilities and elevate your potential to unimaginable heights. You are encouraged to embrace the opportunities that networking and mentorship unlock and watch your goals transform into reality.

CHAPTER 8

PHILANTHROPY AND GIVING BACK

Chapter 8 of "Wealthy Mindset" dissects the profound impact of generosity on those in need and the giver. As the saying goes, "It is in giving that we receive," this chapter exudes the transformative power of altruism. It discusses, in strong terms, why incorporating philanthropy into our lives is essential for developing a wealthy mindset.

To understand the importance of philanthropy, we must first define a wealthy mindset. Beyond mere financial abundance, it includes a holistic approach to well-being and fulfilment. Therefore, a prosperous mindset prioritises personal growth, emotional intelligence, and community engagement.

This implies that true wealth goes beyond material possessions to finding fulfilment through social connections, experiences, and contributions to the greater good of others. Perhaps the most minor thing you should reflect on is that you can never lose your emotional health when you use your wealth to put smiles on people's faces.

Philanthropy- An Extension of Wealth

For many, philanthropy is merely esteemed as a charitable act, but from a wealthy mind's perspective, it is an extension of one's wealth and acknowledging that our resources come with responsibilities. Have you observed that the more people accumulate wealth, the more they are presented with the responsibility to effect positive change in their communities and across borders? This implies that giving back to the society is a noble act. Furthermore, it is a wise and strategic decision for those who aspire to make a lasting impact.

Creating a Legacy

Pursuing legacy is one of the most convincing reasons to practice philanthropy. Dedicating time and resources to charitable causes creates a mark on society that will outlive you and that entire generation. Instead of being self-centred and focusing only on personal wealth accumulation, measure your success by your positive influence on others.

Philanthropy allows you to weave your values into a lasting narrative. The number of people who are inspired by your generosity will also continue the cycle of giving. Thus, you create a legacy that immortalises your name. With philanthropy, your name will never die.

Research has established that acts of generosity are highly connected to improved mental health and well-being. This means that engaging in philanthropic activities reduces stress and increases happiness and life satisfaction. The emotional reward of giving back to society is enough reason for wealthy individuals to make an impact with their wealth.

Moreover, it is crucial to note that giving back is not limited to financial contributions. Volunteering time, sharing skills, or supporting local initiatives can contribute immensely to community development and develop a sense of purpose in citizens.

Philanthropy has the potential to act as a catalyst for change in any society. Individuals can tackle societal issues such as education, poverty, social vices, health care, and environmental degradation through targeted giving and social contributions.

This book encourages you to reflect on what you are passionate about and think strategically about how you can contribute to solutions. Our world needs the contribution of great minds like you. By aligning your resources with your values, you can amplify your impact and inspire others to join the train.

Cultivating a Culture of Giving

To fully develop a wealthy mindset, it is essential to cultivate a culture of giving. However, you don't have to be discouraged because you don't have adequate resources to drive your passion. Wealth is progressive, and you can begin from where you are. In case you do not have enough resources to meet the needs of society, consider starting with family and friends.

This chapter provides practical strategies for encouraging philanthropy in daily life. You can consider simple practices like engaging children in charitable activities, setting up donation programs in various workplaces, or organising community service events that can transform people's attitudes towards giving. Actions like this will instil a sense of collective responsibility to give back to our community.

With the increasing advancement in technology, giving back to society is much easier. Several online platforms make it easier for people to volunteer, donate, and advocate for causes of interest. These virtual resources can empower you to connect with like-minded individuals and mobilise resources to make a greater difference.

Stories of Philanthropists with a Wealthy Mentality

Our world is not short of individuals who have climbed the ladder of greatness and are backing back to their society. The impacts of such individuals are imprinted on the sand of time. History will always reecho their good works and charitable acts.

It is great to explore inspiring stories of philanthropists whose wealthy mentality has led them to positively impact our world. More importantly, we share their stories today, not for head-knowledge sake but as motivations for the continuity of their good works. Will your impact enlist you in the hall of wealthy and impactful individuals?

1. Andrew Carnegie: The Gospel of Wealth

Andrew Carnegie is a Scottish-American industrialist who exemplifies the wealthy mindset through his belief in the "Gospel of Wealth." After building his fortune in the steel industry, he dedicated the latter part of his life to philanthropy. He stated clearly that the wealthy are morally obligated to distribute their surplus.

One of Carnegie's famous quotes is: "It is more difficult to give money away intelligently than to earn it in the first place." He financed the establishment of educational institutions, libraries, and music halls for public consumption. Carnegie ensured that his wealth was instrumental in fostering knowledge and culture. Today, his legacy lives on through the over 2,500 libraries he built across the United States. These facilities continue to serve communities and provide free access to knowledge.

2. Oprah Winfrey: Empowering Through Education

Oprah Winfrey's story remains inspiring for millions of people. She rose gradually from poverty to become a media mogul who exemplifies the wealthy mentality through her philanthropic efforts. Oprah knew the transformative power of education and established the Oprah Winfrey Foundation and the Oprah Winfrey Operating Foundation, which focus on educational initiatives for underprivileged children.

The Oprah Winfrey Scholars Program still empowers young individuals to pursue higher education. This is a beautiful way to encourage a cycle of learning and giving back. Through her generosity, Oprah demonstrates that a wealthy mindset is not limited to monetary contributions. She sees it as an opportunity to nurture potential and create a safe environment for others to succeed.

3. Bill and Melinda Gates: Global Health and Education

Bill Gates and his erstwhile wife, Melinda, founded the Bill & Melinda Gates Foundation. They had the mission to reduce inequity and improve global health and education. Their foundation has invested billions of dollars in tackling diseases like malaria and polio and promoting education in third-world countries.

The Gates believes in pragmatic philanthropy and emphasises the significance of utilising data to drive impact. They believe that "with great wealth comes great responsibility, " which formed the basis for charitable acts worldwide. Our successes should be used to uplift those in need and pave the path for a healthier and more educated world.

4. Richard Branson: Building a Better World through Business

Richard Branson is reputable for his adventurous and entrepreneurial spirit. He leveraged his wealthy mentality to advocate for sustainable business practices and social responsibility. He committed to addressing critical issues such as climate change and social justice through the Virgin Group initiative.

Branson founded Virgin Unite, a nonprofit organisation that tackles complex global challenges and provides innovative solutions. As a capitalist, his approach to philanthropy highlights the potential for businesses to graduate beyond profit generation to driving social change. Branson's story still inspires entrepreneurs to view success through a broader lens, and align profit making with purpose actualisation.

5. Dolly Parton: Literacy and Community Support

Dolly Parton is a country music legend who, through her unwavering commitment to literacy and community service, expresses the wealthy mindset. Her Imagination Library program donates free books to children from birth to age five in the United States, Canada, and beyond. The initiative has distributed over 150 million books and developed the passion for reading and learning among millions of children.

Parton's philosophy is that "the most important thing is to be a good person." This ideology resonates closely with the notion that true wealth makes a difference in the lives of others. It further proves that anyone can contribute to their community, regardless of their financial status.

The stories of these philanthropists illustrate that a wealthy mindset goes beyond the mere monetary value of wealth. It includes the willingness to empower and invest in the potential of others.

Through their charitable efforts, they have transformed countless lives and inspired future generations to adopt a similar mentality.

In essence, a wealthy mindset recognises that true wealth is measured by the impact one makes on the world around them, not by the millions of dollars freezing in their accounts. So, as this chapter concludes, it is imperative to reflect on the true measure of wealth. A rich mindset embraces giving back as an integral component of success.

Remember that wealth is not solely about what we have but how much we share. True abundance is measured by our generosity of spirit, our cheerfulness to contribute, and the legacy we leave behind.

CHAPTER 9

WEALTH AND WELL-BEING

This chapter succinctly discusses the complex connection between wealth and well-being. Furthermore, it unpacks how financial abundance influences our emotional, mental, and physical health and vice versa. More importantly, you are about learning how developing a wealthy mindset can foster a holistic sense of well-being.

Understanding Wealth Beyond Money

We often equate wealth with mere financial resources. However, true wealth includes emotional richness, meaningful relationships, physical health, and a sense of purpose. This broader understanding of wealth reveals that all these elements are interconnected and complementary. They all contribute to our overall well-being, and none is of lesser significance than the other.

Emotional Wealth: Emotional soundness is fundamental to building a wealthy mindset. Our emotions can significantly influence our mindset. Individuals with a wealthy mentality can navigate challenges with optimism because they view obstacles as opportunities for growth rather than insurmountable mountains. This optimism engenders happiness and satisfaction.

Physical Wellness: Physical health is the first and greatest form of wealth. Research shows that individuals with financial stability often have better access to healthcare and balanced resources that can enhance physical fitness. However, wealth accumulation must be balanced with investments in physical health.

Some wealthy people neglect their health while pursuing wealth. Unfortunately, after using their physical health to amass material and financial wealth, they begin to spend their wealth to recover their health. To avoid such a tragic end, engage in physical exercise, eat healthy, and observe mental health practices that boost our bodies and minds.

Social Connections: The importance of relationships in promoting well-being cannot be overstated. A wealthy mindset encourages you to build and maintain strong social connections with others. The support and love from friends and family can act as a buffer against stress and emotional trauma. Social connection is a unique form of wealth that money cannot guarantee. This is why it is great to refine our character in order to accommodate valuable relationships.

The Psychology of Wealth and Well-Being

The psychology of wealth illustrates how our beliefs about money impact our emotional health. People with wealthy mindset develop a positive relationship with money. They see money as a tool that empower them to harness opportunities rather than a source of tension. This balanced perspective shifts the focus from scarcity to abundance and promotes well-being.

Individuals operating from a scarcity mindset often experience anxiety, fear, and lack, which can deteriorate their mental health. Conversely, an abundance mindset encourages cheerfulness, creativity, and a willingness to share qualities that are beneficial to them and their community. However, the abundance mentality must be consciously adopted. As you do, both you and everyone around you will feel the positive impact.

Practical Steps Toward Integrating Wealth and Well-Being

1. **Practice Gratitude**: Practicing gratitude can significantly improve our perception of wealth. Daily, reflect on what you are grateful for, including your financial blessings, physical and mental health and meaningful social connections. This act will

enhance a positive relationship with money and increase happiness.

2. **Invest in Personal Development**: Invest some time and money in personal development. This can include reading books, pursuing education, developing new skills, or engaging in practices that improve mental well-being. Investing in yourself is a primary aspect of a wealthy mindset. It is a good use to sometimes empty your pocket to fill your brain.

3. **Engage in Meaningful Connection**: As you connect with others and share thoughts, ideas, and experiences, you completely deal with feelings of isolation and put depression at bay. Engage in community activities, volunteer, or simply take time to connect with loved ones. This strengthens emotional health and keeps you active and joyful.

4. **Balancing Financial Goals with Wellness**: Although it is crucial to set financial goals, aligning your goals with personal well-being is equally important. Financial success that comes at the expense of health or relationships may lead to dissatisfaction regrets. So you need to strike the balance by

integrating self-care into your financial planning.

5. **Philanthropy and Generosity**: Showing some acts of kindness and generosity heightens your sense of purpose and fulfilment. Philanthropy not only enhances the lives of others but also enriches your life. Imagine how joyful you will be seeing yourself as the source of other people's lifting and progress. The more good you do, the happier you become, thus increasing your overall well-being.

Importance of Health and Happiness

It is pathetic that most people glorify material wealth and set it as the yardstick for measuring financial success and breakthrough. But health and happiness are pivotal to a truly prosperous and wealthy individual. Those with a balanced understanding of wealth know that success transcends monetary gains to the well-being of our body and mind.

The Wealth of Health

Health is often considered the foundation of life. Without it, even the most prosperous individuals may be unable to enjoy their achievements. We can only pursue financial wealth when we are physically healthy. A healthy body can be productive, mentally sound, and resilient against daily stresses.

Again, physical health supports mental well-being. For instance, our physical activities help release endorphins, hormones that enhance good mood. This shows a strong relationship between physical health and emotional wellness. Also, individuals who prioritise their health often report higher happiness and satisfaction in their daily lives.

For everyone who wants to enjoy their wealth, maintaining good health is beyond a choice; it is an obligation. It means that you commit to keeping yourself healthy and acknowledge that true wealth includes the vitality to engage fully with life. Investing time and resources into your health is as indispensable, if not more important, than investing in financial literacy or business ventures.

The Pursuit of Happiness

Many people falsely believe that happiness directly results from external circumstances such as career success, material possessions, or social status. However, true happiness is exuded deep within our thoughts, attitudes, and relationships.

Happiness is always a choice you have to make and take responsibility for. This means fortifying yourself against any situation that may want to rob you of your peace. Show gratitude for daily experiences and enjoy the ordinary events around you. Always think about what makes you happy and be satisfied with what you have.

Additionally, happiness is deeply connected to relationships. Associating with family, friends, and the community provides a sense of belonging. These social interactions enhance emotional well-being and assure us of a support system that is highly needed during tough times. Since love and companionship lead to deeper fulfilment than any wealth can offer, investing more in relationships than in material things is better.

The Synergy of Health, Happiness, and Wealth

Understanding the synergy between health, happiness, and wealth is crucial for developing a wealthy mindset. Practices that enhance health and happiness can unleash the full potential for success in other areas of life. For instance, we are more productive, creative, and efficient when we maintain good health and optimism. With the right state of mind, it is easier to make better decisions, take calculated risks, and get innovative. We need all these essential qualities for financial success.

Furthermore, happy and healthy individuals are most likely to attract positive opportunities and relationships. Thus, they create a cycle of abundance and have an edge over their pessimistic counterparts. With joy and a right state of mind, you become magnetic, inspiring, and exemplary. A wealthy mindset radiates confidence and enhances one's ability to make wealth beyond financial prosperity.

As you pursue success, remember that true wealth is reflected in our ability to maintain our health and nurture our happiness. By safeguarding these elements, you are better prepared to host abundance. Where health and happiness are present, wealth can never be absent. At worst, it will be close by.

CHAPTER 10

MAINTAINING WEALTH

Several individuals focus primarily on accumulating wealth but never learn how to maintain it. Gathering wealth without the requisite knowledge to sustain it will only amount to a waste of time. Such an experience is like fetching water into a basket.

This book would have been incomplete without this chapter. Do you know that the major problem of developing countries is underutilisation and a lack of maintenance strategies? Similarly, a rich person will soon become poor if he lacks the discipline to maintain his wealth.

The skills and mindset required to maintain wealth are highly crucial. This chapter discusses the strategies and philosophies necessary for sustaining and growing your financial resources over time. After amassing wealth, the challenge shifts to retaining and nurturing it in a manner that continues to create value.

Maintaining wealth begins with acknowledging that wealth is not a destination but a progressive journey. A wealthy mindset understands that success requires attention, adaptability, and a commitment to lifelong learning.

Establishing a Growth-Oriented Financial Strategy

1. **Reassessing Goals**: Once wealth is accumulated, revisiting and redefining your financial goals is essential. Do they still align with your current values and aspirations? As life circumstances evolve, your objectives should change, too. So, you should develop a flexible financial strategy to help you adapt your wealth to new realities.

2. **Diversification**: There are better decisions than just relying on a single source of income or investment. Instead, diversify your investments to mitigate the risks associated with market volatility and open multiple streams of income. Understanding your risk tolerance and exploring different investment opportunities, such as bonds, real estate, stocks, and alternative assets, is essential.

3. **Regular Monitoring and Rebalancing**: Wealth management is an active process, not a passive one. As you monitor your investments and financial standing, you will be able to identify trends and make informed

decisions. Rebalancing your portfolio is equally important as it ensures alignment with your current tolerance level and overall financial goals. This way, you provide a safe premise for unprecedented economic situations.

Maintaining wealth requires a commitment to continuous learning. Financial literacy is essential for proper wealth management. Understanding the principles of budgeting, investing, taxes, and market volatility will help individuals make informed decisions that will protect their assets.

"Building a Wealth Mindset: Unlocking the Secrets to Financial Freedom and Abundance" equips readers with the tools and insights necessary to reshape their financial reality. This book reiterates the psychological shifts and practical strategies that can facilitate a significant change in one's economic life.

You must have read that wealth is beyond accumulating money; it is about developing a mindset that attracts opportunities, prosperity, and abundance. This book challenges myths about wealth and wealthy individuals, introducing concepts of abundance and the power of intentional wealth creation. The core principles you have learned are expected to redirect your energies towards a more prosperous mindset, ultimately leading to tangible financial growth.

As we approach the final lines of "Wealth Mindset: Unlocking the Secrets to Financial Freedom and Abundance," remember that the lessons you have learned are to initiate a lifelong journey toward financial empowerment and abundance. The principles this book offers are empty words struggling to find a space in a book; instead, they are tools waiting to be applied in your daily life.

As you embrace the mind shifts necessary to transform your relationship with money, every small change, positive affirmation, and wise financial decision will contribute significantly to your overall wealth journey. Financial abundance is not an elusive dream but a tangible reality you can experience.

So, take a moment to reflect on the insights shared in this book. Commit to action and set a clear intention for your financial future. Begin now by implementing one new strategy, confronting a limiting belief, or practising gratitude for what you already possess. Decide to see obstacles as opportunities, and remember that every step you take brings you closer to unlocking the abundance that is rightfully yours.

Nurture and develop your wealth mindset until it becomes your compass to a life of financial freedom and richness beyond monetary value. As you engage the principles of wealth, you will lead a life overflowing with joy and a profound sense of purpose. Welcome to the atmosphere of abundance!

* 9 7 9 8 3 3 0 3 6 4 5 4 1 *